Spectrum

by

Vivian Khan

Published by New Generation Publishing in 2016

Copyright © Vivian Khan 2016

First Edition

The author asserts the moral right under the Copyright, Designs and Patents Act 1988 to be identified as the author of this work.

All Rights reserved. No part of this publication may be reproduced, stored in a retrieval system or transmitted, in any form or by any means without the prior consent of the author, nor be otherwise circulated in any form of binding or cover other than that which it is published and without a similar condition being imposed on the subsequent purchaser.

www.newgeneration-publishing.com

 New Generation Publishing

Foreword

This eclectic collection of new poetry by Vivian Khan reflects various aspects of her wide range of interests and life experiences. A countrywoman, raised in a remote part of Wales, her enduring fascination with wildlife at home and abroad shines from the pages.

Her interest in other countries and cultures is evident. With a lively imagination and in a free style she paints glowing word pictures of her overseas travels, capturing significant moments with insight and clarity.

The anthology is ideal for browsing and will intrigue and delight readers of all ages and from all walks of life.

Christine Chadbourne.

This book of poetry is dedicated to my late husband, Dr Barrie Khan, and to my family who have always loved, cared for, and supported me.

I am greatly indebted to, and my sincere thanks go to a dear friend, Christine Chadbourne, for being a very forthright critic.

Contents

Moon Gold 1
Early morning view from a fifth floor hotel window in
Blackpool... 2
In Memory of Aberfan 3
Digging.. 5
Angry Waves 6
Pure as Gold 7
The Oriental King.. 8
Walking Man.. 9
Red and Black 10
The Cottage Garden in Penrhos, Gwent 12
Farmyard Moggies 13
Mawu and the Rainbow Snake 14
Sunset 16
The Heron... 17
Owls Hunt 18
Goldie the Goldfish 19
The Hedgehog 21
Bridge over the River Swat, Kalam Valley, Pakistan...... 22
The Stubble Field 24
Puffin Appeal 25
The Deserted Home in Wales... 26
Fungi.. 27
The Bicycle Rickshaw driver 28
Memories of the Poor's Lane, Penrhos 31
The Chai Khana......a teahouse 33
Middleton Lake 35
A Regal King.. 36
Dedicated to Ann... 38
A Day at the Rookery 39
Blue Tits 40
Quartet... 42
Senses 43
Hunting the Hare 44
The Tightrope Walker 45
Gale force - the Coventry Road, Birmingham................ 47

Swallows	49
Rage against War	50
Pain	51
The Mole	52
The Old Pear Tree	53
Death of me, a Snowman	55
Scenes from the North Yorkshire Moors	56
Street View	58
Always - In memory of Barrie	60
Mr Toad	61
Beneath the Sea at Devil's Crown, Floreana	62
The Chestnut Tree	63
The Bird Scarer	64
Onset of Autumn	65
Captured	66
Memories	67
Remembrance	69
South Stack, Anglesey	70
The Pearls	71
Iron monster	72
The Parrot	73
Birds	74
St Editha's Church Bells	75
Powindahs	76
The Caves of Drach	79
The Spirit of the Jungle	81

Moon Gold

Gold.
The moon sweeps across the sky,
pale and round,
flying high.

Gold.
The moon passes behind a wispy cloud,
soft, enchanting,
veiled in a shroud.

Gold.
The moon's beauty is a brilliant jewel,
inspiring authors and artists
of many persuasions and views.

Gold.
The moon gleams the whole night through,
with a sparkling silvery gold colour
of palest hue.

Gold.
As from a pirate ship,
the full moon changes shape over a long time,
becoming a crescent lip.

Gold.
The moon is no longer seen;
to numerous exotic far off lands,
she sheds her beams.

Early morning view from a fifth floor hotel window in Blackpool

Wispy cobalt grey clouds edged with
glittering silver
moved very slowly
across the pale sun streaked morning sky,
like old tired horses endeavouring to gallop.
Icy cold, muddy chocolate brown waves
rolled far distant from the shore,
their white frothy spray
leaping and recoiling,
venturing to the flat sandy wasteland.

A tall stick pin woman,
huddled in a bright red fleece,
strode purposefully against the penetrating wind,
her old faithful bulldog
waddled patiently along beside her.
Far out on the edge of the crawling sea,
one lone, red billed, oyster catcher moved,
the long beak probing for morsels,
a few large, flying, dipping and diving herring gulls
screeched petulantly.

Suddenly the scene was lost,
sea mist descended rapidly.

In Memory of Aberfan

The catastrophic disaster occurred in Aberfan, near Merthyr Tydfil, on 21st October 1966, killing 116 children and 28 adults.

High, very high,
the colliery spoils tip stands,
black, menacing, stark and bare,
its conical head pointing heavenwards,
soon there was
a valley of despair.
Crack!
rumble
tremor, frantic shudder,
earth loudly moaned,
suddenly boulders, stones, mud,
dirt came rolling.
Gushing forward
blackened water,
oozing earth,
the speed ever increasing,
never ceasing
never ceasing.
A thick crawling lava like mixture
encompassed
a school building,
it could not resist,
or withstand
the onslaught.
Scared children were running,
bodies were squashed, flailing, flying,
tossed, all screaming
'Mummy! Daddy! Help us, help us we are dying.'
Suddenly there was an unnatural, brooding, un-nerving complete silence.
No shouts, no screams, no moans, no groans,

only the stunned weeping of the parents.
Their children, God's children, all had disappeared,
they had been gathered home.

Digging

He was bent, with spade gripped in work worn hands,
digging in his garden.
The steel spade glinted as he dug it into the sweet earth,
he loved the smell of the crumbly reddy brown soil,
the sight of the pink wriggling earthworms trying to escape
from the phenomena of daylight,
the chirpy robin redbreast that quickly flitted onto the spade,
eyeing quizzically the newly turned sod,
looking for a quick meal.
He straightened his bent back; pain etched his drawn furrowed face.
'Give in,' his mind tells him, but pride is strong,
'Never,' he mutters softly,
his spirit will not be daunted.
With newfound energy he grabbed the dirty old brown sack from nearby, tipped it,
out rolled the King Edward seed potatoes, pinkish in hue,
he planted them, one by one onto the prepared rows,
diligently covering them with the brown fragmented moist earth.
This was a labour of love.
The work of the day complete,
spade over shoulder, he hobbled slowly home
to sit, dream awhile, make a cup of tea,
may be sleep.
His thoughts mused on the garden,
and turned to the vegetables that he wanted to plant,
the exotic flowers he would love to grow.
A dream. He wondered if the dream would ever become a reality.

Angry Waves

All day the cold angry waves
battered the shore, brutal,
cruel as the squawking herring gulls, whose beaks stabbed and grabbed
at unsuspecting meaty prey,
whilst they were blown to and fro by the arctic winds, to the rhythm of the waters roar.
Grey, slate grey, the waves curled and crashed and ever cried,
the bubbly spray shot high to soak those wrapped up human beings, bent and cold,
who dared to walk along the prom.
On such a wild and devastating day
boats bobbed up and down, hither and thither, at the mercy of the fast dashing waters.
The tinkle, tinkle of the yacht pennant holders, like dainty bells, were the only joyous sound,
yet tinged with a sense of urgency to be rescued from the tempestuous storm.
All day, unceasingly, the cold angry waves battered the shore.

Pure as Gold

when the cold dark streets
grew empty
there came a sweet trembling
piping sound

like the lonely mystical note from a sitar
it rippled
through the narrow alleyways of
old Agra town

it enveloped everything gently
like the sleeping monkeys on the roof
caressed mountainous stalls of various wares
invaded the piles of colourful fruit

it quivered over resting rickshaws
murmured around curled up sleeping men
trembled outside a broken window
then slid unnoticed quietly in

the sound sighed and sobbed
a sitar rested against the wall
suddenly there was total relief
a sense of eternal peace

the piping sound pure as gold
silently crossed the room
the sound and the sitar rejoiced
joined and became as one.

The Oriental King

He strutted across the verdant pasture,
pecking here and there,
he did not have a care.
His beautiful colourful plumage glistened in the cold,
sunlit, early morning air,
pillar box red, shimmering green, a dash of white,
natural fawns, flecked with deeper tones.
This pheasant gave so much pleasure to passers-by,
as he strolled peacefully around the field.
Unfortunately, espying an opening in the bushy roadside hedge,
he strayed from his kingdom to a roadside patch,
exploring the broken bracken, twigs, leaves and rampant rough, coarse grass.
Suddenly stark consternation,
he wanted to return to the field.
The constant traffic roar so close befuddled him.
Frightened , his sense of direction had completely gone,
he made a wrong panic movement.
The oriental king lay dead upon the grey, gritty, gravel road, limp, crushed,
his glorious plumage fluttering softly in the wind.
A flashing speeding metal box had taken his life;
the green field space is so completely empty now,
that strutting beauty gone forever more.

Walking Man

(based on the legends from the Pima tribes in Arizona)

In the beginning was a place
of water, darkness and dust,
from that came Walking Man,
into a black, dark world he was thrust.
He took the grey dust and sluggish water,
began steadfastly to roll a mighty ball.
"It's time for me to create the world,"
he shouted, the echoing, reverberating over all.
"It's too dark for me to see this place that I have made."
He shook water droplets from his strong, sinewy hands;
dramatically shining, lemon coloured stars formed a cascade,
winking brightly in the night sky, dancing like ribbon bands,
but Walking Man still could not see.
So capturing starlight, clay and water,
magically a pale moon
was formed from all three.

The silvery moon and twinkling stars shone in the sky,
but sight still evaded Poor Walking Man.
Filling a huge pan to gather water and Moon Glow
entrapping them…a moment of wizardry, flashing began.
He caught the strange exotic rays and threw them so high
a round gigantic, orange, fiery sun was birthed to fly.
The dark world turned into a lovely bright light,
Walking Man, for the first time, could see
high white topped mountains that stood like church spires,
far stretched patchwork fields and forests green.
Blue oceans crawled, rippled, with waves sometimes crashing,
limpid lakes and gurgling wending rivers could be seen.
Delighted with the world that he could see now,
thankful and always singing praise,
Walking Man was as happy as he could be,
he wandered the Earth to the end of his days.

Red and Black

She sat thinking of her sister, she hated her
because she was all that she had aspired to be.
She had fame, fortune and was wildly free.

Rage ran through her, red, fire red rage,
consuming her into the black depths of despair.
Why did her mother love her sister more than her? It was not understandable, not fair.

She imagined that her mother would love her best,
that she would be sexy, witty, funny and very clever.
In her mind her mother would have given her unconditional love and be with her forever.

She saw herself starring in films, the red carpet down, flashing cameras,
her name in bright lights in the West End, attending first nights,
swinging parties, best champagne, travelling the world,
the future was so very bright.

Then her stick like arms reached up, sharp scissors in hand,
slashing movements were made, her red sticky blood drained down the wall.
She laughed hideously; she had just seen her sister fall.

She saw herself in the large ornate mirror,
Queen Elizabeth for a day, crown, ermine cloak and sceptre in hand,
leaving Buckingham Palace, riding in the gold coach along the Strand.

A tall dark handsome man, her psychiatrist, came into view,

sheer rage, red blood and deep blackness whirled around in her brain. She hated him.
The next moment she thought, 'I will get ready to star in tonight's West End performance again.'

The Cottage Garden in Penrhos, Gwent

It is heavenly to be in my Welsh cottage garden
now that springtime is here,
the sheet white snowdrops hang their dainty heads,
and brilliant sparkling jewelled crocuses appear.
The beautifully barked viburnum bush
stands elegant, with sparkling pinky white bloom,
greeting miniature ice blue muscari,
dispelling winter's dark satanic gloom.

Creamy, waxy jasmine petals
shine forth like a myriad of miniature stars,
even the bright pheasant eyed narcissi dance
in the breeze, as though to the jazzy music playing from
New Orleans bars.
The double white hanging aubrietia meets
trailing butter gold alyssum,
laden bright pink tresses of the American currant bush,
respond to the warming rays of the spring sun.

Hosts of large King Alfred daffodils
stand stately, tall,
overshadowed by the large yellow bright forsythia tree,
near to the red brick wall.
The heavily flowered branches trail
with such gracious ease,
this garden is a colourful scented treasure,
it cannot fail to please.

Farmyard Moggies

There are so many moggies in the farmyard,
drinking fresh creamy warm milk from a large old tin pan.
They are large, small, tattered, very thin or over fat,
silky black, tortoiseshell, bright ginger, multi-coloured, snowy white or tan.
There is Gringo, an arrogant huge ginger stripped tom,
he thinks he is master of all he surveys.
However Rhoda, with the slinky gold green eyes,
has a plan for his downfall one of these days!

Winnie, a part Persian Blue, with very hooded eyes,
fancies old grey paunchy Buster, who is fat.
Sadly Buster has a crush on Thumpolina, a dainty,
white, seductive number, with one black paw, a very beautiful cat!
As fate would have it he is not in her mind,
she thinks Gringo is superior, fearless, fantastic and fun.
So she tries to attract his attention, rubbing slowly against him,
however he breaks away into a fast run.

Now Magwitch, a big black brute strolls away from the others,
he's going to spar with the toffee nosed ginger tom.
He's decided to draw blood, give him a beating by biting and scratching, and to send him away from the farm.
There are so many moggies in the farmyard,
characters every one.
Each like a human being, with hopes and dreams,
desirous of love, companionship, food and fun.

Mawu and the Rainbow Snake
(Based on myths from the Togo and Dahomey people)

Nothing was in the world,
all was gloomy, grey, bleak and bare,
only Mawu, the Creator Spirit wandered
dreaming of what could be there.
When the long strange dream had ended
Mawu suddenly sprang to life.
Time began. What would he do?
Create a world free from strife.
He took the yawning emptiness,
rolled it firmly, strong and bold,
a Rainbow Snake was born,
with flickering black tongue and eyes of gold.
Snake and Mawu together formed the world
with flat land and unmoving sea,
bored by the utterly silent stillness
they chose to indulge their creativity.
Rainbow snake dug trenches, rivers flowed,
Mawu piled stones for the mountains high,
filling them with gold and precious stones,
creating vast forests, green fields and an ever changing sky.
Over creating was a problem,
slowly the land began to sink.
Mawu called the Rainbow Snake to help him,
"You can hold the world up, I think."
Rainbow Snake twisted and coiled himself
three thousand times around the earth.
It is said he is still there
supporting the land to which he gave birth.
Coils speedily moved through the oceans,
sometimes they moved the stars and planets in the sky,
scales flashed as radiant, brilliant lightening,
another coil became a pretty rainbow able to fly.
Rainbow Snake was ever changing

from white to shades of angry hue.
If he should shudder very badly
can you guess what Earth will do?

Sunset

An orange glow fires the sky,
old sun is burning bright.
Who would think that it's near to sunset
dusk creeping, the onset of night.
Mingling with the passing changing clouds,
the sun gently begins to drift away,
a ghost like fleeting moon awakes,
heralding the end of a sunny day.

Darkness begins to softly fall,
charcoal grey bats start to fly,
their shapes are sharply silhouetted
against the background of the darkening sky.
The sun slips beneath the skyline, far away,
gone is the last streaky golden ray.
Is it promising to be back tomorrow?
Will it bring another hot, sun filled blazing day?

The Heron

Beside the sunny open rushed pool in the green grassed field
the wise old grey heron stands, one legged, still,
still as can be,
sometimes like a statue, sometimes moving. A living creature
hunched, with head and neck drawn into the shoulders,
looking miserable and abject.
A sudden swift movement, with two feet solidly on the ground
the heron thrusts the energised body forward,
the long piercing beak, like the mythological sword
Excalibur, strikes strongly into
the calm clear water.
The glistening fish, terror ridden, trapped in the dagger like
yellow beak is wriggling for its very existence.
Sinuous, swallowing neck movements occur rapidly,
an exaggerated, near flapping wing movement assists the
snake like neck.
Immense gobbling movements occur,
the poor struggling fish is no more,
merely a morsel in the now swollen belly of the heron,
who calmly stands again on one leg ,
waiting,
watching motionless for the next victim.

Owls Hunt

Through the long night watches
owls spread their wings,
speeding on their journey,
owls wings,
owls wings.

The owls search the long night through
for mice, voles, small rats, even a succulent shrew,
such tasty morsels, so good to eat,
owls meat,
owls meat.

The morning dawns, the owls screech,
return to their tree tops and to sleep,
the world awakes the day to greet,
owls sleep,
owls sleep.

Goldie the Goldfish

Why can goldfish be sold in plastic bags with little water?
Why is there no animal welfare protection from the crazy life many are forced to lead?

Who would be Goldie, a bright goldfish?
He is swimming crazily around in a thick glass bowl, which is placed on a wooden window ledge, in the sun's rays, day after day.
The water temperature changes several times according to the heat from the orange papery sun,
but the gold fish has no chance to escape from the terrible conditions, and no rescuer will come.

Nothing seems to change for Goldie,
he's like a dervish, spinning forever round and round, endlessly moving in the small confined space,
never able to be free.
He's captive for a day, a week, a month, a year , maybe it will be two or three.
Strange unintelligible shapes float through the patterned water bowl,
merging, glittering, reflecting, light contrasting and expanding en masse.
The colours are sometimes gloomy, grey like turgid water, or rainbow colour, iridescent bright,
disturbing and ravaging poor Goldie's vision,
causing all the shapes to split, crack and have divisions.
Slight relief sometimes arrives in the form of crumb like food,
he gobbles it greedily, but in pensive mood.
Danger is afoot; Pongo the family ginger cat has decided to have a game,
with nimble paw he trawls the water, he always behaves the same.

The dread of the cat's paw making contact, of becoming a cat's meal
is terrifying, so he twirls, bends, twists, turns and reels,
until he can rest momentarily safely on the bowl's sandy bed.
There's just a split second of peace within Goldie's crazed head.
Then the same ceaseless pointless movement begins again, round and round, round and round,
 it's making him psychotic, driving him insane.
What an utterly monotonous, cruel, and beastly existence.
Goldie has to go on, swimming in a confined glass bowl forever,
day and night,
for the rest of his life.

The Hedgehog

Sitting in the quiet garden on a well worn oak bench,
the mind was dwelling on days long, long spent,
of vegetables grown to exhibit in the local village show,
enormous onions, leeks and several varieties of both white and red potatoes.
Intrusively, a snuffling noise disturbed the thoughts, but nothing could be seen,
I peered around the garden in the direction of the soft burbling stream.
Avidly listening , the sound was heard even more strongly again,
then some leaves were moving in the direction of the old metal covered garden drain.
Who or what was there was a mystery,
then from the heaped leaves a small shape appeared,
a brown eyed, long nosed, spiky hedgehog, with such very tiny ears.
He spotted me, he stopped dead in his tracks, frozen, not knowing what to do,
not wishing to frighten him, I sat absolutely motionless too!
We gazed long at each other, the hedgehog,
on his short legs, began to move,
he positively hustled away to a nearby dark green leafed laurel bush as quickly as he could.
I wonder if I will ever see that little snuffling hedgehog in my garden again.
It was a short encounter but his image will always remain.

Bridge over the River Swat, Kalam Valley, Pakistan

High up in the mountains, with the mighty towering snow covered peaks of the Himalayas all around,
a gushing turquoise icy river rushed over huge stained boulders,
under a crisp snow covered glacier, to emerge as a wide ribbon of water, wending its way amongst the stamp sized patterned agricultural fields,
far down into the valley of Swat.
An unshielded rope swing bridge of uncertain years,
with wooden slats placed unevenly apart, straddled the rolling water.
The slats moaned, squeaked, creaked and groaned as they moved crazily from side to side by the wind force,
like untrained performers, dancing wildly.
This bridge was the only way for the locals to cross the untamed flowing river.

A farmer, a tall man, with a rifle slung carelessly across his back,
dressed in salwar and kameez, topped by a black waistcoat, and with a tribesman's hat on, started this journey, clinging perilously to the rope.
In places his hands could not touch both the rope sides of the bridge,
reliance was on his balance.
Tentatively he edged his way nervously across the bridge, perspiration rolled from him despite the icy wind,
he could feel the old, rotting, broken slats beneath his feet.
As a young nimble lad he had travelled over this bridge so easily, but now middle aged there was stark fear in his heart,
it was beating madly... bump... bump; he was sweating even more profusely.
A slight sudden movement, the rope breaking, a foot put wrong on the slats, he would be lost to the world forever,

falling, to be dashed like a limp doll onto the gigantic boulders,
to slide to a death in the sub zero, icy blue, freezing water,
the cruel, penetrating, blinding, cold wind whipping him as he fell.

Contrastingly a brilliant sun spread glowingly across the broad valley,
almond trees were just starting to bloom pink, heralding a late spring of greenery and lushness.
It was an inhospitable, beautiful, landscape high up in the shadow of the Himalayas,
but a much loved homeland to the farmer crossing the bridge over the river near Kalam.

The Stubble Field

A gaggle of Toulouse geese marched upright from the farmyard, soldier like,
in a line, to the stubble field where the tall golden wheat once stood.
They were joined by raucous rooks, twittering starlings and stout pigeons,
all bustling to pick up the dropped wheat grains for food.
The field was alive with activity and noise,
it was greater than any traffic roar,
 the birds failed to notice the approaching silvery steel coloured plough,
drawn by an enormous new green John Deere tractor.
Suddenly a loud screaming call erupted from one of the geese,
pure anxiety and sheer panic set in all around.
Quickly the sky became dark with a moving black cloud of startled birds,
the geese half flying, half running, wings beating made for their pen, surging across the ground.
All the stubble and loose grains slowly and completely disappeared,
to be replaced by a ridged, furrowed, terra cotta red ploughed earth sheet.
No more grain for the geese, they will have to rely on the farmer feeding them.
No more grain for the birds, they will have to search elsewhere for their food.

Puffin Appeal

The bright eyed perky puffins have a variety of local names,
'Coulter neb', 'Bottlenose' and 'Sea parrot' around the coast of wild Northumberland,
'Pope' or 'Popey duck' in the rugged North Cornwall villages and towns,
Tomato Billed Razorbill in its far flung Mediterranean wintering grounds,
Nori in Orkney and Shetland,
Lundi in faraway Iceland,
Tommy Noddy by some local fishermen and
Fratercula artica, in learned natural history tomes.
Puffins appeal for their colours and bustling stance,
they are considered cheeky, charming dazzlers,
upright smart suited dandies,
with brightly coloured rainbow beaks,
oversized funny clowns, with big orange feet.
Earnest as parents,
they nest in the soft, sandy, thrift clad hillsides close to the sea,
usually one brown, fluffy, downy chick hatches out, and is making demands straight away!
With bills crammed full of small squirming fish
cleverly held crosswise, heads and tails aligned,
the parents fly in and out of the burrow
all the day time.
The pufflin grows quickly, abandons safety, and heads to the sea,
relief is felt by the parents...at last they are free!
Puffins are the most beautiful amazing birds,
full of character, stylish, always busy and bright,
they are considered one of nature's most endearing sights.
Sadly they are becoming an endangered species,
for everyone, saving their environment is an essential fight.

The Deserted Home in Wales

There's no curling smoke rising from the chimney,
no sound of laughter coming through the door,
there's no furniture left in the parlour,
there's no carpeting covering the floor.
No hand has cleaned the windows,
they're streaked with dust and grime,
there is no smell of delicious cooking,
everything has gone with time.
I stand by the old kitchen door and remember
precisely how it used to be,
my beloved mother, my dearest father,
we were such a happy loving three.

Fungi

Down in the dark, dismal, dank woods, autumn has arrived,
for naked trees with bare branches stare heavenward to the sky.
Decaying leaves lie on the sodden woodland floor,
once so colourful, golden, shaded red, brown - they are no more.
Fairy ring Champignons grow through the lifeless leaves,
showing their small, pointed caps beneath the gaunt, skeleton trees.
A dreadful sickening odour invades the icy air all round,
it's from the foul smelling jelly of the white stalked Stink Horn fungi,
standing completely alone on the earthy cold ground.
Long stalked Parasol mushrooms, from their thick mossy green bed reach,
edible blue grey Oyster fungus grow out from a huge tree, a beech.
White spotted, on brilliant orange scarlet, the distinctive Fly Agaric can be seen,
bright, bold, beautiful... the fungi queen.
The Horn of Plenty grows underneath a sprawling spreading tree,
dark brown, funnel shaped, camouflaged, it is not easy to see.
The Sickner, hiding under the spruce, can cause bad vomiting,
its very pill-box red colour sends out a warning.
A patch of bent, broken bracken near the old oak scarcely hides,
the lethal Death cap with its tri-poisonous inside.
Dying, a sturdy birch plays host to Orange Spot, Candle Snuff, Cramp Ball and Puff Ball,
the dank wood is home to amazing interesting fungi of all sorts.

The Bicycle Rickshaw driver

Jostling for position many rickshaw drivers patiently wait,
as the unsuspecting tourists step outside the Agra Hotel gate.
All are shouting in various tones, 'Sahib, you will get best price from me.'
A quick choice must be made to get free from this rather frightening melee.
Agreeing a price, two eager, anxious tourists mounted an ancient rickshaw,
the man, skinny, tall and sinewy, pedalled as fast as possible, away,
weaving in and out of hooting tu-tus, honking taxis, horn blowing buses, slow moving camel carts, scooters, cars, miraculously he found his way.

There were very agile monkeys jumping along the walls and swinging in the trees,
some were sitting grooming themselves and their young, picking out their fleas.
Huge scavenger vultures languidly circled overhead,
eyeing the ground meticulously for anything that was near dying, or already dead.
Dhoti clad men carried wares on shiny pseudo silver trays,
colourful sparkling bangles, bracelets with shimmering stones,
soft pure silk scarves, heavily scented perfumes, glinting gaudy necklaces,
small and large hair slides, displayed on very elaborate black velvet cones.

Fruit stalls lined the roads, such attractive artistic displays,
lime green and blushing red apples, sweet smelling guavas and puce plums,
large oranges, yellow pears, bright red scarlet strawberries,
fruits ,which had all been ripened by the ever present warming sun.

A vendor pushed his wonky barrow, there was a brass engraved samovar in pride of place,
small, less than clean, glasses tinkled as he pushed through the throng,
'Chai 'he calls happily,' Chai chai,' it sounds like a repetitive song.
The tourists remembered the words 'Delhi belly-upset tummy'…so they passed along.

There were side streets, unmade roads, the rickshaw perilously dipped and dived,
the tourist's backs were aching; they were thirsty, sweaty, and clammy hot,
there were clouds of fine red dust and ceaseless noise.
Their spirit of adventure was dampened for today and a return to the hotel was sought,
the smells, sights and sounds of Agra had already made
an impression that would never be lost.
The rickshaw driver somewhat crest fallen sadly obeyed the request,
pedalling slowly, he had lost his initial zest

He knew that there would not be any more work today,
so wearily he turned along Music Street and engineered a crafty delay.
He invited his customers to alight and go into an air conditioned shop,
the owner welcomed them, seats were offered, and tea was proffered in clean china cups.
The sound of that wonderful enigmatic mystic instrument, the sitar, was heard,
a live impromptu concert began; all was peaceful, calm and undisturbed.
Grateful, relaxed happy tourists emerged into the hot afternoon sun,
the rickshaw driver made his way slowly through the growing crowd, his work nearly done.

The Agra hotel came into view, he wondered if he would get the agreed rupees,
notoriously tourists jumped off the rickshaw and ran away with such ease.
The tourists alighted, their faces wreathed in happy smiles,
'We've had a wonderful time, seen so much, and you have pedalled us for miles,
'We'll book you for ten o'clock tomorrow morning .Is that alright?'
'Yes!'
They gave double what he asked for; he was crazily happy, and filled with delight,
he felt elated, filled with joy;
suddenly everything in his life was very bright.

Memories of the Poor's Lane, Penrhos

An ivy overgrown tumble down stone cottage lay on the right hand side of the wide entrance to the grassy Poor's Lane,
part of a wall with a broken chimney pot
was all that really remained.
Cheeky challenging jackdaws and rooks enjoyed flying around and perching atop,
it seemed like a game with them, vying for who could sit on the favoured spot.
Some villagers claimed that a headless rider
charged along the lane at nightfall on a huge fifteen hand high white horse,
others told of a mighty powerful black dog with huge red eyes,
which jumped out, killing and eating any passer by, of course!
As children we were terrified to go near the place at night, however it was a children's playground,
nature's paradise in the friendly daylight.
In spring the hedgerow's new bright green leaves replaced winter's gloom,
stark bare hazelnut trees had 'lambs tails', three centimetres long.
Delicate yellow, golden eyed primroses grew in clumps along the way,
groups of bright pink primroses with orange stamens gave a very bright display.
A carpet of butter gold celandines bloomed, like sparkling brilliant stars,
specimens of the hairy, pale green stemmed goats beard grew on small raised earth bars.
A lone cowslip plant peeped above the grass, its dainty shaped flowers trembling like tiny bells,
Dog's mercury grew in abundance all along the lane, intermingled with bluebells and the growing leaves of the poisonous henbane.

The tall grey green rough barked oak trees were perfect for climbing up, so high,
a child could become Tarzan for a while, with a rope, swinging wildly upwards to the sky.
What fun! Who would fall off? Who could swing for the longest time?
We ran, we chased, and we jumped over the stream backwards and forwards,
 splashing water and sometimes falling in.
Paddling our hands in the cold running water, we caught 'bull heads',
tiny wriggling brown fish, only to let them go again.
The Poor's Lane provided endless hours of adventure, freedom, and wonderful fun,
it is now a precious golden memory of a childhood long gone.

The Chai Khana……a teahouse

This was a real teahouse discovered on my travels in a wild and desolate area in Pakistan. .The
'chai' was most welcome!

A young dishevelled brown eyed, black haired, shoeless boy, no more than nine years old,
tried to attract the sparse passing traffic.
Shouting and waving the Pakistani flag and holding a huge metal teapot, he was doing his best to get custom for his father's teahouse,
to earn a few rupees, to eke out a hard life in an unforgiving land.

The chai khana or teahouse was a roughly made wooden shack on the stony hillside, off the winding road to Kalam.
Here wild goats, of various sizes and colours,
 scrambled nimbly over huge grey boulders,
eagerly foraging for food amongst the scrubby bushes.
Scrawny scavenging vultures flew high overhead,
eagle eyed, waiting to spot any carrion that was near dying or already dead..
The climb up to the tea house was steep and difficult, but the views were idyllic,
breath taking.
Towering snow covered, sharp pinnacle mountains of the Himalayas stretched, never ending, like sharp needles,
soft edged cotton wool clouds rolled, tumbled and pranced across a turquoise blue sky like acrobats,
the air was sharp, biting, and bitterly cold.
A tumbling rushing icy mountain stream hurried through the teahouse cutting it in two,
an extremely wobbly moving dangerous plank bridged the two halves together,
 A warm welcome was given by the owner, with much smiling and hand shaking , in the traditional way.

Colourful home made cushions of different sizes lined a long settee,
guests were encouraged to kick their shoes off, to lie back and relax , to leisurely wait for their tea.
An ancient brass kettle hissed and spluttered as it boiled on the smoky wood fire, which was kept alight with freshly cut scrub.
Soon prettily decorated handle less small porcelain china bowls were filled with steaming hot, sweet green tea,
spicy vegetable samosas were offered for refreshment.

Everything was moving in the quaint room in the tea house ,
small bells, fabrics, hangings, the smoke, and the flames,
even the wooden planks that formed the shack,
seemed to sob and sigh, as the screaming wind passed through them.
Tthe roof planks jittered and joined them in unison.
It was as if everything was intricately moving together, crying out against their circumstances.
However this lone teahouse , together with the welcoming host
had provided a most welcome rest,
from the stark harshness that was the winding gravel road that led to Kalam.

Middleton Lake

Middleton Lake, a place for quiet reflection and solitude,
is a beautiful wide expanse of water, ever changing as time goes by,
one minute bright, dappled, sparkling with sunlight,
next, dark, cold, rippling, reflecting the altering light of the greying sky.

There's time to watch the natural things of life in their changing moods,
the sleek, black feathered, white billed coot pottering near the rushy edge,
dabbling in the browny- black oozy mud.
Further out across the lake a long necked crested grebe suddenly sprang up and dived,
then appeared as if by magic in a different place,
movements executed with such balletic grace.
Far away lay a bull rush bed, where a few rotten logs lay,
three hunched grey blue herons perched, looking like huddled, miserable old men, dejected, still.
The reality was that their eagle eyes were watching for an unsuspecting fish passing by, they were ready for the kill!

A small raft of tufted dusks swam near the middle of the lake,
proud males displayed their shiny black feathers, white flanks and a significant drooping crest at the back of the head,
dark brown females were obscured by such brightness and swam unnoticed towards the water lily beds.
A sudden glint of blue passed as a kingfisher darted by,
busy long tailed tits wove their way through the scrubby hazel trees at the waters edge.
Circling high up in the sky, a broad winged buzzard called,
a robin sang from a nearby tree,
a group of fast moving common terns flew and dived, falling like stones, then skimming the water.

A Regal King

A large grey beast, all of ten ton, came down the winding sandy path,
a powerful African bull elephant of mammoth size,
he had nobility, a stark kingly regalness , dignity,
as he passed amongst the bilboa trees, rough thorny scrub underneath the blazing bright blue, cloudless African sky.

His massive trunk swung quite rhythmically and gracefully from side to side,
the large pendulous ears moved to and fro, swotting flies,
he strode at a pace that was very fast.
A party of tourists sitting nearby, very quiet and still, in a safari truck,
hoped the magnificent animal would go, without incident, past.

His curly lashed, yellow ovoid alert watchful bright eyes seemed small for such an enormous animal,
the ivory tusks were curved, long and yellowed with age,
the gait was direct, extremely purposeful,
abruptly he turned off the path into the scrubby maze.

There he sprang into action, having located a tall, large trunked leafy tree,
within seconds it was felled, crashing heavily, noisily to the dry cracked ground,
the amazing strength and magnificent power of the elephant was a pure delight to see,
raising his head, he gave a blasting loud trumpet that resounded all around.

Soon other elephants appeared and proceeded to enjoy chomping the greenery,

there were several endearing young babies, mothers, a herd, a very large family.
They ate nosily, in total harmony with their surroundings, then, bellies full, the family slowly sauntered peacefully away.
Wherever he would take them in the vast and changing African plains , the herd followed their beautiful, gigantic leader.

Dedicated to Ann

A dear friend and my daughter's mother in law,
she will always be missed.

She was full of life, laughter and fun,
then dark days came and she was on the downhill run.

My dearest friend was so very very ill,
she was slowly passing away.
The unmerciful cruel cancer tore at her very being,
excruciating pain, was sucking her life blood away day after day.
She could fight no more the mind-blowing pain,
morphine came into play; pain relieving but dulling the once so active brain.
Words were muddled, incoherent, whispered but unheard, thoughts unspoken.
Lips moved, formed shapes,
hallucinating in a lost world.
There were fragmented broken images,
barely audible memories fleeted in and out indistinctly,
she tried to focus, remember her dearly beloved sons, other family members, grandchildren, weddings, friends, holidays, laughter,
all so dearly loved but slipping away from her.
She lay motionless in the bed, eyes closed, looking as if she had already departed this life for a sweeter life beyond the stars.
The breathing was laboured, becoming more difficult with every small gasp.
Her sons held her hands tenderly, we all kissed her.
One last big sigh…she was released from her terrible pain and suffering at last.

A Day at the Rookery

It was an early cold morning,
bitter winds were fiercely blowing,
a pale weak sun peeped over the horizon
to a low temperature of minus three.
The flat uninteresting landscape was enhanced
by a group of tall, threatening, leafless trees,
where high up in the topmost branches,
a large number of grey- black beaked rooks
were clinging, almost unbalanced, in the strong breeze.
There were displays of nodding and bowing, of beak touching,
of shiny feathered black rooks flapping their wings
up, down, up, down.
The usual loud cacophonous caw caw cawing exploded,
as each baggy trousered rook tried to attract attention with their sound.
It was January, and having managed to gain a partner,
came decision time; to repair last years nest or build new.
Choosing a branch to build on caused much dissension,
then the usual interminable social abuse reared its head and grew.
There was pecking, strident caw cawing and beating each other away,
for each pair thought the other had the premier building spot,
and stealing other birds partially started nests occurred several times a day.
Industrious rooks looked for suitable materials, but
there was bullying and fights over the perceived best strong twigs.
Finally the day drew to a close, darkness descended,
the sun sank away, and then a glowing full moon shone brightly in the sky.
Activity ceased, the rooks huddled on branches like huge black bats,
sweet silence fell upon the rookery, night would pass.
At daylight squabbling and caw cawing would start all over again.

Blue Tits

The wooden nest box hung on the creosoted garden fence waiting for the blue tits to arrive,
soon two swiftly landed, peeked in, flew away, then returned,
entered the box, feathers slightly ruffled,
they were so energetic, bright and alive.
A nest was made from dried grass, small feathers and moss,
it took them several days,
then five small dainty eggs, streaked with browns and bluish greens were laid.

The long wearying days of sitting began,
naked, blind new babies would hatch in about two to three weeks.
Both blue tits would share this arduous time consuming labour,
they were only waiting for the nestlings from their shells to peep.
Trouble started as soon as the young hatched,
the greedy raucous babies were always demanding food.
The parents laboured from dawn 'til dusk
providing juicy worms, fat grubs and termites,
gathered from the birch wood.

The parents became tired and bedraggled,
the once brightly coloured feathers became dowdy and very pale.
The noisy nestlings were feathered, large and over spilling the nest
ready to try their wings and go solo…
hopefully they would not fail!
Out of the box they successfully scrambled,
each of the five launched into a hazardous first wobbly flight,
they all managed to reach a strong branch to perch on,

independence gained; they proceeded to be noisy and quarrelsome , indulging in a sibling fight.

They still required their parents, but quickly grew up, separated and went their own way,
the parents recovered their liveliness and their bright plumage
the rhythm of their lives, mating, nest building and
 rearing young will be the pattern of life
for the rest of their days.

Quartet

Spring, the season of slow awakening,
dainty snowdrop heads bow glistening white,
glorious frothy forsythia and daffodils with waxy yellow petals shimmer,
scented large pink, white and blue hyacinths stand like sentinels,
such a heart warming sight.

Summer comes with all its glory, blue skies and fleeting clouds,
the sun's hot rays envelope the very receptive cold ground,
tall spikes of multi-coloured lupins, elegant blue delphiniums,
black eyed, blood red poppies and Sweet Williams
perfume the garden air around.

Autumn creeps in quietly, shrouding the trees with a soft mist,
the leaves have changed from green to shades of honey brown,
clumps of Michaelmas daisies, golden rod and dark bronze chrysanthemums
now decorate the very many different gardens,
with their attractive flowery crowns.

Winter brings the biting cold, flurries of snow, ice and rain,
the red holly berries shine brightly, its also mistletoe time again,
leaf covered gardens look sleepy like hibernating toads,
only the beautiful waxy pure white Christmas roses,
appear alive, in the weather, which is so dreadfully cold.

Senses

Feel the smooth yellow skin of the ripened William pear,
the sharp prickles of the hawthorn bush,
the light caress of a falling snowflake,
the silky stem of the tall brown headed bull rush.

Hear the cattle bawling from the old cowshed,
the cheery song of a nightingale in June,
the noisy honking of Canada geese as they fly overhead,
the wind gently whispering through the pink roses in bloom.

Taste the purple skinned sweet fresh Turkish figs,
the salt spray of the sea on your lips,
the delicious ladyfinger and aubergine curry,
the syrup made from the red rose hips.

Smell the Tibetan roses in a monastery garden,
the herb garden of rosemary and thyme,
the wood smoke from the twigs and leaves burning brightly,
the bark of the tall swaying pines.

See the crowing cockerel ruling the roost in the farmyard,
the clouds of starlings that darken the evening sky,
the outline of stark trees on a winter landscape,
the migrating Bewick swans flying on high.

Our senses are essential to us,
from the moment we are born,
they define us as individual persons,
our likes and dislikes form.

Hunting the Hare

A hop, a skip,
the big brown hare was running away,
the dogs were following
in full bay.

Leaping, bounding ,
the hare was worn,
tired, overcome, distraught ,
without the shelter of a home.

The hunting hounds closed in
with sharp noses to the ground,
the hare rolled over, no mercy,
he was found.

Treacherous fangs and sharp claws
tore in on the hare, ripping away,
what a dreadful death,
what a cruel display.

Is it necessary to hunt wild animals of any kind
for this horrendous so called pleasure?
Is it necessary to behave with such vile cruelty
to animals, that as a nation, we should treasure?

The Tightrope Walker

High in the sky a tightrope was stretched between two points
over a turbulent muddy river, which was rushing over boulders,
spewing water and foaming, far far down below.
Excited crowds had amassed on either side to watch a spectacle.
A clock sonorously struck two, its sound reverberating all around,
Suddenly all was hushed, deathly silent ,not one sound.
Black clad , dressed in an all- in- one Ozzy stepped out,
in his mind he was emulating Charles Blondin
and the Great Farini who walked on a tightrope over Niagara Falls.
His first foot met with the tight rope,
gingerly the second foot went in front of the first.
No safety net to protect him,
he inched across the space,
mind concentrated, heart beating rapidly,
not a whisper from the onlookers,
they hardly dared to breathe.
Would he fall? That was the unspoken question on everyone's mind.
He was edging very slowly along,
palms sweaty,
think, concentrate, think, concentrate,
his mind hammered those two words.
He was sure that time had stood still,
a quick furtive glance showed him
the ordeal was nearly over.
Soaked wet with perspiration,
near terror set in,
slow, keep nerve he tells himself, slow, slow.
He left the tightrope with a lithesome spring,
success, seemingly endless rousing rapturous applause followed.

He waved to the gathered crowds … he loved the adulation,
he was victorious,
he was a champion,
he would have a place in history,
but he knew that the spectre of cold death had stared him in the face.

Gale force - the Coventry Road, Birmingham

The cold wind skipped, played and frolicked around,
leaves danced and whirled down the street with a zingy sound.
A large, long haired, furry ginger tom cat, padding along,
was blown from side to side,
twigs, ripped from the trees, went on a roller coaster ride.
The wind rippled through women's long skirts ballooning them out,
whizzed under very short ones, embarrassing the owners, causing them to shout.
Women clad in abayas became voluminous as the wind filled their clothes bulging them out and in,
people dressed in salwar and kameez shivered, trembled, as the cold wind blasted through their clothes, to their skin.

It zipped under the men's hats,
lifting and sending them to roll along the street, so very, very fast.
Women's hijabs of all colours and shapes were pulled from their heads with a swift twirl,
trouser legs flapped, unbuttoned coats became like parachutes, ready to fly their owners away in a whirl.

Fruit stalls toppled, plastic buckets rolled, shutters rattled, windows jittered, doors banged to a close,
Advertising boards crashed heavily, broken in bits,
the wind was tearing away at gale force six.
Plastic bags and cartons were swept up, looking like pale ghosts when swirling high up in the sky,
huge bins lurched, rolled, their contents spewed out all over the ground,

tins clanked merrily, jumping and diving along the street, making a rhythmic sound.

The wind was really exhilarated at the havoc and mayhem it had caused on this day,

as quickly as it had started, the mischief was over. The wind subsided and went away.

Swallows

Balmy flower-scented days,
the bright sun breathes warm on the old, terracotta red brick barns.
Tall pink, black spotted foxgloves grow, their bells turned downwards,
close to the hedgerows in the field nearby.
Ox-eye daisies, white, with a startling yellow eye,
grow along with pure gold buttercups amongst the lush bright green grass.
The orange throated swallows with their long forked streamer tails,
dip and dive, skimming gracefully across the meadows and streams,
feeding on small insects as they fly,
miraculously they never seem to land.
Arriving from South Africa for nesting,
acrobatic and skilful, these summer visitors
return to last years nesting places,
where the barn's wooden rafters meet the worn brick walls.
From the mud they gather, miracles are created,
distinguished nests of such artistry and perfection,
with the tiniest hole for entry appear.
The summer passes; the air is getting an autumnal feeling,
with their new families, the swallow's urge to return home is great.
They all gather together on the telephone wires,
twittering away as they sit a while,
contemplating the long return flight.
Suddenly they are all quiet,
as if they have received a signal.
In unison they fly noiselessly away.

Rage against War

The tongue is mightier than the sword it is said, so
let peace talks take the place of aggression and
rage, rage against the wrongs of war,
for men weep and die and are no more.
Their lives they have given for what was deemed a noble cause
but reasoning reminds us no such thing is true. For what is war?
It is a few powerful people's view upon a situation,
and they demand that all shall fight for their belief.
But where are they? Yes, missing from the battle,
ensconced in a safe place, a retreat.
Rage, rage against all war before it is too late,
preach peace talks, conciliation, a communal road, for
the politicians rarely die from bullet wounds, from being shelled or bombed.
They are not called to kill and maim other people's sons,
they will not return from battle wounded, crippled for life,
unable to walk, to run, to enjoy a normal family life.
Many souls remain incarcerated because of their traumatised mental state,
their lives have been ruined, ravaged, tattered, and broken.
Rage, rage against all forms of war before it is too late.

Pain

Pain
comes in waves,
hot and cold
shivering and shaking
shattering sight,
searing , shooting,
breaking the mind into a thousand pieces.
Swimming into unknown realms,
swamped into nothingness,
wispy, misty,
haunting images tormenting,
nagging , nagging,
the memory has vanished
wandering in a land of nothingness.
A t last the pain is receding,
no more ghostly shapes are seen,
back from the land of oblivion
to face again
the world of lucid beings
thankfully without
Pain.

The Mole

The mole has an amazing kingdom,
well below the surface of the ground.
There's a maze of subterranean tunnels that turn and twist,
so that Mr Mole, who has poor eyesight, cannot easily be found.
He pushes the soil with his strong, spade like, clawed paws,
the black velvety, close furred fellow makes an above ground earth mound,
Those tramping above may only observe a loamy 'molehill,'
a silent chap, the mole, hardly ever makes a sound.

With his pink sensitive nose he seeks out juicy worms,
storing some in his special larder for a rainy day,
like other moles he usually lives alone,
in a very monastic secretive way.
It was not always so for the mole population,
for Queen Alexandra ordered a coat made of mole fur.
This signalled it was acceptable for people to catch them,
suddenly they were endangered; to buy their skins was very dear.

So started a trend going on through the ages,
until animal rights groups decided it was inhuman and cruel.
By popular demand synthetic fur became fashionable,
on the world famous catwalks it replaced the real.
Moles now live in relative safety,
masters in their own special underworld.
It's generally a lonely existence,
hunting , eating , sleeping and remaining totally undisturbed.

The Old Pear Tree

In the early evening when the light begins to fade away
the giant pear tree, silhouetted black against the sky,
comes to mind.
It stood proud and strong, warrior like, throughout the year,
surrounded by long feathery grasses of all kinds.
Bedecked with pure white waxy virginal bloom in springtime,
 tiny green pears, so perfectly formed, soon grew.
Later the branches of the tree drooped heavily,
with large ripe Pitmaston pears of an orangey yellowy hue.

Gathering the magnificent smooth skinned fruits was an art in itself,
for mother hated bruised or blemished fruit in any way.
A master of inventiveness with pear recipes,
the house was heavy with the scent of cooking pears
every day.
Sticky sweet jam, smooth luscious jelly, hot spicy pickle, tasty fruity chutney,
all were stored carefully in many, various sized glass jars.
Clearly labelled, dressed in red and white gingham, neatly tied with string,
they awaited the famous annual competitions at the local village bazaars.

Other pears had fallen and were smashed upon impact with the hard ground,
stripy, black and yellow wasps, the occasional large hornet,
and lots of glossy, gossamer winged flies flew headily around.
Drunk and exceedingly lazy on the sweet syrupy juices,
persistent droning and buzzing was their only sound,
slow laborious crawling was their only movement,

some had even rolled upon their backs, dead when they were found.
The Pitmaston pear tree will always be remembered,
it was part of my youth, so many decades ago.
I am sure it is not standing proud and strong any longer,
age will have taken its deadly toll.

Death of me, a Snowman

This poem is dedicated to Olivia,
my nine year old grand daughter

I was tall, strong, firm and bright,
a big giant ,on the landscape, which was white.
The black trilby hat distinguished me
from the other snowmen that I could see.
My long coat trimmed with thick brown fur
and the red woolly gloves had caused quite a stir.
I stood so proud on the cold, cold night,
not knowing what was to happen in the morning sunlight.
Alas! My nose it began to drip, drip, drip,
the hat, at a jaunty angle to the floor began to slip.
My legs were wobbling and wobbled away,
the fine top coat sagged to my dismay.
Tiredness came, my strength deserted me,
my head was somehow sinking down below my right knee.
I knew that my life was slipping fast fast away, going, done.
I had fallen victim to that early morning bright sun!

Scenes from the North Yorkshire Moors

The moors stretched as far as the eye could see,
vast space, huge skies, all untamed, beautifully free.
Sharp craggy rocky outcrops rose up on this undulating land,
unseen dangers lurked, quagmires and bogs,
which acted in the same way as sucking shifting sands.

The bell heather, purple ling and cross leaved heath,
like vast textured purple -red tufted carpets clung to the gravelly thin soil beneath.
In the soft whispering breeze patches of woolly cotton headed grass were as pristine white as a pillow,
close to a tinkling stream stood a small crooked trunked tree with branches of tufted catkins; a 'pussy' willow.

Tart cloudberries and blue- black juicy bilberries grew on shrubs nestling near a clump of red berried rowan trees.
A big hare appeared; jumped out from a nearby tussock of grass and, sprinted across the terrain with such lithesome ease.
The greeny yellow curling sphagnum moss, spongy to walk on, covered much of the ground,
edged with flowering long and short sedges, a peaty brown water bog was found.

Bog asphodel was growing, displaying a myriad of waxy star like flowers,
close by the carnivorous sundew plants also grew,
their roundish green sticky haired leaves were endowed with supreme powers,
for insects who alighted on them disappeared, they were swallowed as prey.
Close by several timid grouse poked their heads above the grass, ducked and quickly scuttered away,

A skylark flew from off the ground, trilling, winging its way, ascending, lost in the sky,

two majestic buzzards, savouring the thermals, soared effortlessly high in the clouds,
Amongst the golden furze the chirr of a linnet could be heard,
on a mossy overhanging rock perched a wheatear, a very distinctive bird.

The sun changed; it was almost sliding away, pale white,
the moors rose like soft golden wings in the special late evening light,
the crescent shaped new silvery moon came into sight.
An owl hooted; there was the bleating of sheep, far away,
then complete silence. Night.

Street View

Lean rats, fat rats, old rats, young rats search amongst the broken, rubbish filled black plastic bags,
hunting for food.
Skinny cats, ginger cats, black cats, caterwauling cats prowl amongst the black, broken, rubbish filled plastic bags searching for food.
Black dogs, brown dogs, patched dogs; mangy curs
roam amongst the black broken rubbish filled plastic bags
delving for food.
All are unloved, unwanted, desperately hungry and unfed,
they are looking for any scraps of food; chips, masala fish, and bread.
perhaps, half eaten chicken, beef burgers, or curried rainbow rice
they care not if the food is full of spice.
The harsh bitter wind sweeps strongly around,
last nights spent chicken tikka boxes, fish and chip wrappers,
and various branded plastic bags abound.
Some are whirling skyward, like upward shooting stars,
others roll round dancing over shoelaces,
or fly over the rooves of cars,
some add decoration to the trees in the nearby park
others just lie, discarded in the dark.
Windswept piles of litter gather in shop way closed doors,
or are swirling and tumbling across the pavement's dirty floor.
The weakly rayed sun sinks beneath the darkening storm clouds,
night quickly descends, black, enveloping as a shroud.
Strains of Indian music from a newly opened restaurant are loud,
shisha smoking men huddled in brightly lit Arabic cafes abound.
There's the mouth watering smell of curries and barbequed food,

in the little coffee bars people are laughing and talking in happy mood.
However on the street it appears to be just the same,
the lean rats, fat rats, old rats and young rats still scurry,
the skinny cats, ginger cats black cats and caterwauling cats crawl like hunting tigers over rubbish filled plastic bags in a great hurry.
Sniffing noisily and poking their noses into the broken bags
are even more black dogs, brown dogs, patched dogs and mangy curs!
All are still unwanted, unloved, desperately hungry, searching for food.

Always - In memory of Barrie

I hear your footsteps on the crunchy gravel;
see you sitting in the comfortable fireside chair,
hear you run lightly up the red-carpeted stairs.
feel you running your fingers through my hair.
I look at the many photographs,
talk to you in my mind for each and every day,
where ever I may wander,
you are close by, never ever far away.

Your coat still hangs in the wardrobe,
along with your favourite shirt and tie,
the pipe and tobacco pouch are still in the study,
the faithful old dog by your favourite chair lies.
The ancient leather midwifery bag and much used stethoscope
repose with your many medical books—untouched.
Your voice still echoes, whispering, through the house,
my darling you are always missed so very, very much.

Mr Toad

In a small hollow of an old rotting stump of a sycamore tree,
on the shreds of yellowy decaying wood, near to a well of uncertain age, surrounded by dainty blue wood violets and shamrock there sat a common toad,
still, still as a statue, not the slightest movement.
Its posture suggested it was smug, pleased with itself, satisfied,
almost a touch arrogant,
even the mouth appeared to have a half grin on it.
Unhurriedly it began to move,
right hand, left foot, left hand, right foot.
The broad squat body was like a melting patchwork of colours,
browns, olive greens and grey tones.
Warty looking dry skin covered the toad,
bulbous eyes looked straight at me,
the parotid glands were clearly visible at the back of the neck.
I considered the situation,
here was a once in a lifetime opportunity.
Without thought I reached forward and picked the creature up gently and firmly,
there was no struggling. My fingers gently stroked the skin.
Observing the toad, the inward panic of the creature transmitted itself to my hand,
immediately I returned the toad to the stump.
Promptly it crawled to the well, threw itself in and disappeared,
only the ripples across the water caused by the toad's entrance remained.
Stroking the toad and the feel of the toad in my hand was an interesting experience,
The feel of the toad's skin will always remain.

I wonder what the toad thought about the experience?

Beneath the Sea at Devil's Crown, Floreana

Lowering herself into the water from the boat
she swam a little way, then
lying spread eagled on the lapping waves of the Pacific Ocean,
close to the island of Floreana.,
with snorkelling equipment on,
she looked down into the water.
Beneath was a huge depression,
like a bomb crater, not harsh or stony,
it was covered in bright green sea grass, marine algae and
frondy strips of browny green seaweed,
this waved in tune with the ocean current,
it was such a wonderful and beautiful scene.
A large, lone, green turtle
with jagged edged jaws grazed peacefully, cutting the greenery,
his strong mouth quickly gathering the food.
The small bright eyes were perpetually watching for predators,
legs were flipper like, broad and flattened, aiding swimming,
the colours of the turtle ranged from black to dark olive
brown, with individual markings on the domed shell.
A huge eagle ray came into view and glided past, shoals of
bright blue and yellow King Angel fish, Amberjacks and
Balloon fish swam hurriedly by.

She stayed gazing at the wonderful
spectacle….mesmerised,
the sea was so alive… time meant nothing,
here was a magical world the like of which she had never
encountered before.
A tap on her shoulder … her responding movement….
the observed turtle swam away… the moment was broken.

The Chestnut Tree

Tall, statuesque, alone she stands,
the spreading chestnut tree,
her candlesticks of pink and white
shine forth for all to see.
Such dainty flowers cluster there
on tender stems of green,
some half hidden by giant leaves,
are only partially seen.

Days pass, the flowers die,
their petals tumble down,
swept along by the breezes strong,
the tree has lost its brilliant crown.
Small prickly conkers, begin to grow,
green skinned, rotund, rough,
sun drenched, rain soaked,
the skins are getting very tough.

Summer days, blazing, glowing,
come and pass away,
now the mature large conkers
wait for dewy autumn days.
Soon they come mellow, misty,
the ripe conkers fall to the ground,
their prickly cases split asunder
as they shatter with a plopping sound.

Chestnut brown, shiny, smooth
untouched, the conkers lie,
until excited children discover them
as they walk close by.
They're gathered quickly, much treasured,
many different conker games will be enjoyed.
Who will have the king of the conkers
out of all the girls and boys?

The Bird Scarer

In the middle of the furrowed Long Meadow
bent and wind blown, a scarecrow stands,
clothed in farmer Nick Morgan's cast off clothing,
baggy trousers, oversized jacket, so he has no hands!
Made of rough wood, padded with prickly, weather beaten straw,
a simple lop-sided cross forms the scarecrow's frame,
an oversized stained trilby protects the old head
from hot sun, snow blizzards, hail and driving rain.

He is supposed to be scaring the birds far away,
protecting the newly planted wheat seed every day,
he is clearly ineffectual as clouds of birds all noisily land,
gobbling the seed, which was not the farmers plan.
Flocks of noisy starlings darken the sky in their flight,
stout garrulous rooks join them to roost until morning light,
the moon begins to glimmer, silvery in the twilight,
the scarecrow still stands, hopeless at his job and a frightening sight.

Onset of Autumn

The hazy sunshine beamed through a cloud stained azure blue sky,
bees droned drowsily around the pink Michaelmas daisies,
sucking the last of the nectar from the blooms.
A lone peacock butterfly flitted slowly from the buddleia bush in dizzy flight, seemingly unsure of where it was going; maybe it was a last flight before the onset of
ice cold days and certain death.
The once golden fields of swaying wheat, barley and oats were now reduced to stubble,
The first migratory geese loved this as they delighted in roving, in relative warmth, enjoying searching for the last shed grains.
Trees subtly changed, their leaves becoming like an artist's palette, full of shades of yellows, reds and browns.
In towns people still rushed on their never ending pattern, working, shopping, amusing themselves,
aware of the seasonal change taking place with Mother Nature only by the mannequins in the fashion house windows,
dressed in stylish autumn clothes.

Captured

He paced and paced and paced around
the same circuit, day in day out.
People came to stare at him,
sometimes they rattled the cage bars and shouted unintelligible things,
it mattered not to him; it did not mean a thing.
At last, he lay upon a concrete slab, the sun was beaming bright.
he laid stretched full length to reveal beautiful white, golden and black stripped fur,
his noble head was magnificently marked, his beautiful golden eyes were ever watchful.
In his mind he recalled the days when he was free
living in a paradise, a deep green jungle, where he wandered freely stalking his prey.
He remembers his brothers and sisters, his mother and father,
the day when they were all captured,
the banging noise, his parents killed,
his separation from his siblings who were all put into different cages,
the terrifying darkness that he was locked in, angry voices,
what seemed like an endless journey without food and water,
his near to death arrival to his current cage.
He knows the life that he had has gone forever.
Wearily he rises from the slab, and wanders the same well worn path,
this has become his daily life ,he is doomed, never again will there be freedom,
only death will bring him relief from this hell…this cage.

Memories

Asalam a laikum. Peace be unto you.

When I am dwelling in the smoke laden English city
that is bleak, grey, damp and unkind,
memories of my far away homeland village,
come unbidden to my mind.
Tear drops from my ageing eyes,
they course down my dark wrinkled cheeks,
for the images that repeatedly appear,
are of my family and friends, who were and are so very dear.

Sometimes I am watching the jewel of morning light,
listening to the throaty crow of a cockerel in the yard.
My mud flat roofed house was a glorious palace
rich in humanity, caring, bright, and alive.
The smell of roasting spiced meat invades my senses;
it was not chips and more chips everyday,
there are memories of chicken curries, BBQ meat, dal, samosas,
delicious curried vegetables,ladyfingers, purple aubergines and orange peppers,
all cooked on the outdoor oven beneath the sun's strong rays.

I played with Ayesha, Rashid, Mohammed and Maryam,
my sisters and brothers,
from dawn until dusk.
there were heavenly blue skies, a lush beautiful landscape,
we enjoyed ourselves very much.
We rode a huge fearsome camel through the fields for a couple of miles to fetch water each day,
the camel snorted and spat when we attempted to put the deep brown goat skin bags filled with water on its back,
it misbehaved on the pathway returning home for all of the way.

Images of leading the huge black buffaloes to pastures new,
herding the multitude of varying coloured goats
from the village pen to feed,
watching, shepherding them,
the whole day through,
returning them safely home at twilight are precious.
Chatting with friends over small wood fires deep into the night,
until the last embers died down are deeply, lovingly held in my heart.
It was possible to just roam and roam,
there was freedom and safety for everyone everywhere
all around the home.

Why did I get sucked into this western world?
I came for opportunity, a better life.
It has been forty five long years,
time to reflect on life's struggle and strife.
I long to see my childhood home again,
I can only pray,
that Allah grants me this wish one day.

Asalam a laikum. Peace be unto you.

Remembrance

His hands lay unmoving on his lap,
the twisted arthritic fingers gnarled.
In lucid moments he remembers how they used to be,
strong, sinewy, well groomed, and most of all pain free.
He remembers playing ball as a child,
using his hands to climb up and swing on the trees,
clinging to a thick rope and swinging in Tarzan style over
the fast running brook with such ease.
He had somersaulted, cart wheeled and swung on a trapeze,
held his wife's hands tenderly, his fingers entwined with hers.
tenderly caressed his new-born baby son
all so far back in time… so many years ago. His hands had
hewn wood; a wood carver he held chisels, saws and planes.
He had carved intimate details on so many different
carvings putting on finishing touches to please.
His mind flashed to the bright red car he had driven, taking
his family all over the countryside.
painfully, with an aching heart he momentarily remembers
that he is alone now for both wife and son died.
He ponders on what has happened.
How did his hands get into such a state?
How did he get so old?
It all seems to have happened so quickly.
He tries to remember what he has been thinking about,
but…it's all lost, gone…
He sits, forlorn, with hands unmoving,
with fingers twisted and racked with pain.
He is waiting …….for what?

South Stack, Anglesey

Granite grey, menacing, silent, gigantic ,
the Pinnacles of South Stack like sentinels stand.
Protectors of the glorious, windswept, pink thrift covered rocks, defenders of a naturally wild and beautiful land.
Some times to gently kiss the feet of the awesome stacks,
the wrinkling, sunlit, sparkling sea crawls.
At other times the roaring black blue, curling waves rush
to crash thunderously against the ancient slate walls.
Big, fierce beaked, fat sleek herring gulls
loudly squawk, hover, dip and whirr.
Pretty, periously perched kittiwakes screech and gabble
as jostling, shoving, pushing guillemots on their ledge
create a raucous stir.
There is a 'Look out' with telescopes and binoculars to view,
the vast and interesting colony of seabirds , the whole year through.

The Pearls

It was her birthday party on Friday evening,
she wore the necklace around her smooth swan like neck
exhibited for all to see. Expensive, lustrous antique pearls fastened by a marcasite clip.
What could their history be?
She thought not of where the pearls had come from, the Indian Ocean, the Persian Gulf or the Red Sea,
Were the pearls gathered from the cold blue ocean floor
or from at turbulent lake or crawling river bed?
How many slave divers had risked their lives from daring hostile creatures for the pearls, or succumbed to the dreaded bends?
What difference anyway?

She smiled to the entire gathered crowd, enjoying compliments galore, preening, parading, simpering,
showing off the pearls that were bought by a besotted admirer.
They were creamy, cool, almost translucent against her skin.
The party was getting noisier, strident music blared away,
already it was yet another day.
Her fingers touched the enchanting pearl necklace lovingly, still entwined around her long slim neck,
the pearls from a country far away.
The necklace possibly means nothing except a status adornment,
just another piece of jewellery to be cast off,
dumped, discarded thrown. Maybe it will be worn again just as thoughtlessly. Maybe she really loves the pearls.
Who can say?
Her body language gives nothing away.

Iron monster

The chugging iron monster wrecked havoc,
creeping; crawling arms worked, abusing, chewing, tearing everything in its way,
the hedgerow now stands strangely silent, the birds quickly flew away.

Branches of the willow, silver birch and hawthorn are relentlessly torn asunder, sap dripping, the wood crying,
screaming like the victims of a bloody war.
Twisted, bleeding, sighing . dying, the once strong, proud, budding branches are no more.
They are gobbled, swallowed, churned around ,spat out, spat out:
leaf and twig compost now.

No more the greying, yellow tufted pussy willow catkins,
no more the long dangling 'lambs tails' of the hazel tree,
no more will fresh new buds open to greet the warm spring days,
the tender blades of new green grass are shattered, maimed,
the bright yellow celandines are squashed as if run over by a train,
the bed of dog's mercury lie bent, massacred.

Bruised, beaten, battered, broken, mangled murdered,
the once so beautiful hedgerow is now unsightly ,its radiance lost.
And why?
Is it to satisfy the requirements of some petty rules made by faceless 'officials'?
Is this how we should be taking care of our environment today?

The Parrot

The parrot sits upon his perch, encaged, with both eyes closed,
however voices he can hear,
muttering, whispering, and spluttering.
'You know that parrot,
 He is such a silent, quiet, attractive bird?'
The parrot thinks unto himself
there will be a shock one day,
I'll watch and look and quietly observe
what those fools my masters say.
'Look at his glossy green feathers.'
'What a lovely bird again today.'
'Is he any bloody use?'
'Should we pack him on his way?'
The parrot listens, amused, for he knows
the day is coming when
their misconceptions will be shattered, for he'll squawk,
squawk and squawk again.
Their comments will be very different,
'Shut up you bloody parrot!'
'We've heard enough of you,'
'Your squawking gets on my nerves.'
'Let's make a parrot stew!"
'I'll sell him on the market.'
'Give him away now today.'
'The bloomin parrot ain't no good,
who taught him to speak anyway?'
The parrot now knows he has won the day,
for listening to their voices he can make
them sweetly soft, petting, ordinary or roaring angry,
for by squawking or not
he has sealed their fate!

Birds

The house sparrow sits upon a green bough,
the trilling skylark flies above,
a yellow beaked male blackbird rustles in the bush,
on the sycamore tree there is a collared dove.
A cheeky robin feeds upon the crumbs
spread by the kitchen open door,
his red breast is plump and very puffed,
he cannot eat any more.

An acrobatic blue tit swings and hangs aloft
upon the washing line.
Why is he always upside down,
his song a chattering rhyme?
A speckled breasted thrush rests in the old pear tree,
warbling aloft a beautiful song,
suddenly the wings beat down toward the ground,
an unsuspecting snail is swooped upon.

St Editha's Church Bells

Tamworth's parish church dates back to Saxon times,
when Tamworth was the capital of Mercia.

Oh, hear ye now the plaintiff toll
of St Editha's muffled church bells.
Their mournful toll
reaches far and near.
St Editha's church bells.

Oh hear ye now the sweet, joyous peel,
of St Editha's delightful church bells.
Their heart warming sound
encompasses everything around.
St Editha's church bells.

Oh, hear ye now the beautiful different tones
of St Editha's church bells.
Their blessed, bright varied tones
reach as far as the village homes.
St. Editha's church bells.

Oh, hear ye now the sacred Sunday sound
of pealing, ancient St Editha's bells.
They call the people to God's home,
ringing cheerful   praises of their own,
St. Editha's church bells.

Powindahs

It was early morning , the chill of the dawn,
no heat from the red ball rising in the sky.
In Dera Ismail Khan I stood on the well worn wide sandy pathway beside the slow, brown often sluggish Indus river, as it snaked
its way through the town like a twisting ribbon.
I was eating hot vegetable samosas, curiously waiting to see what was going to come by.
There was a sudden noise and a long camel caravan of some fifty camels came into view, a moving mass of legs and necks.
The camel master was leading followed by the camel puller who always had the unenviable job before travelling of seeing that there was a wooden peg in each of the camels nostrils,
 tying a rope around it ,and securing it to the following camel,
until all were tied in a controllable chain.
Whilst being famous as 'ships' of the desert, they were known for being exceedingly bad tempered animals too.
Loading the camels was also very difficult as each camel had its own complaining way
if the load was not balanced properly,
or it was too heavy
they howled, snorted, lay down kicked and refused to move, despite cajoling, for the rest of the day.

As the huge camels passed by the curl of their thick lips, which helped them graze on thorny scrub bushes, could be seen,
extra long curled lashes protected their eyes from occasions when there were sudden sand storms, blizzards and driving rain.
The sweaty heat from their bodies gave off a peculiar odour and their slobbering was plain to see.

One knew not to get in their way for their pure animal
strength was frightening and intimidating,
they were solely intent on their pathway.

Small children, the sick and the old, baskets of cockerels
and hens, tools and tents rode high up on the camel's
backs.
Not visible were the bales of cloth, spices and jewellery,
the trading goods of the powindahs, they were hidden by
coarse jute sacks.
Walking purposefully,
beautiful dark haired, silver jewelled women with
costumes of aubergine coloured cloth,
were protectively flanked with big ferocious fighting dogs.
Dark eyed, armed, moustached men, stood tall and proud,
keeping an ever keen watch all around.
It was usual for the local youths, who did not like the
powindahs, to cause trouble to erupt by
jeering, leering and making rude remarks and sounds.

The powindahs were heading towards the old wooden
swing bridge. I could here the clattering noise as they
crossed.
It was a dangerous death defying journey but
they needed to get to the fresh grazing lands across the
river,
the animals could then feed on the undulating hillsides
pastures of lush green grass.
The men and women could set up their black tented homes
and rest for some days,
with the ferocious dogs guarding the territory along with
watchmen.

This was the dangerous wild pattern of life,
a centuries old way that suited them.
With family guides they had journeyed , without
compasses or maps, from the foothills of the Himalayas,

to spend the winter, on the much warmer Indian Plains

Now summer they were returning back to their beloved homeland,
for cooler weather, to rest ,and prepare for the same long hazardous journey southwards again.
Their caravan master would shout and raise his stick,
the camel puller would chain the camels,
the camel caravan would be on the move …. ……again.

The Caves of Drach

as seen on March 6th 2001

Running, jostling, pushing, hassled anxious faced
crowds gathered in the afternoon sun.
French, German, Dutch, Swedish, Spanish,
but my friend and I speak only the English tongue.

A barrier was lifted. Shuffling like herded sheep,
the crowd began to slither away, disappear,
down deep. Into the yawning cavern they vanished,
an artificial light glimmered so there was no undue fear.

There were startling magnificent, unbelievable shaped
stalagmites and stalactites
shining, sparkling, their icy shapes encouraged the
imagination to roam, a dragon's head,, a wizened old man,
a grand palace, even sea waves with the curls of foam.

Our minds thought back over the hundreds of years
it had taken for such stupendous sites to appear.
Hidden from the world until comparatively recently,
a breath taking, unbelievable scenario was about to occur.

Bright artificial lights revealed an ice blue lake,
unfortunately tourism and money greed had its way,
an unseen voice echoed all around the cave,
'Be seated… a spectacle will be played out now, today.'

The lights went out, silence, you could hear a pin drop,
faint sounds of classical music haunted the air,
a lighted boat with a small orchestra aboard glided across
the lake,
no sound from the oars, the concert was a beautiful
magical heart stirring affair.

All eyes were focused, each lost in thought, the emotion of the moment,
I sought the comforting warm hand of my dear friend.
This was a real time happening
played deep down in the bowels of the earth.
Sadly but necessarily it had to end.

The Spirit of the Jungle

In the far Ecuadorian rainforest
the spirit of the jungle took me by the hand,
heady, entranced as a seasoned opium eater
dazedly I wandered through the golden green, steamy
unexplored land.

Cobweb like mist enshrouded the soaring canopy,
rain suddenly hurtled from the cloud torn sky,
beating on the head like piercing nails, sharply stinging
the burned skin, like bites from a very poisonous fly.
Changing quickly, strong rays from the searing fiery sun
blazoned,
a wild cackling cacophony of bird sounds arose,
the screeching of Amazon Green Parrots,
sweet songs from some Scarlet Crowned Barbets,
the crazy chatter of colourful Red and Blue Macaws,
with disharmony from a couple of Aracaris
embroiled with a group of Violaceous Jays.
Long tailed blue black Anis flew in line formation and
Band Tailed Pigeons perched in the trees.
Harsh shrill calls from the featherless, blue faced,
spiky crested primeval looking Hoatzins,
vied with the lone stark cry, from a huge Turkey Vulture
soaring overhead.
Troops of Red Howler Monkeys swung and leapt
effortlessly from branch to branch,
and a curled up sleeping Sloth perched near the top of a
tree in a branch bed.

Like leeches on human skin,
brightly coloured orchids clung to their hosts,
Strangulatory plants curled
and twined around stalwart trees,

covering them like thick overcoats.
Preying Mantis and Stick Insects abounded,
frogs of all sizes, colours and shapes ceaselessly croaked.
Owl eyed butterflies and the striking blue morpho flitted about,
long nosed bats, cleverly camouflaged, clung to a slim broken post.
The crawling waters held engaging endangered species,
slimy slithery Water snakes, Pink river dolphins, and huge Paiche fish.
At night the Caiman, crocodile like reptiles, appeared on the muddy river banks,
two enormous eyes glinted through the darkness of night,
then a loud splish splash into the water ,
as a light from a tourist boat, or hunters, came into sight.

The spirit of the jungle has taken me by the hand,
Time is spent in dreaming of returning
to that wild unbridled
steamy Ecuadorian rainforest land.

www.ingramcontent.com/pod-product-compliance
Ingram Content Group UK Ltd.
Pitfield, Milton Keynes, MK11 3LW, UK
UKHW042000230426
12048UKWH00009B/457